CHELTENHAM
THEN & NOW
IN COLOUR

SUE ROWBOTHAM & JILL WALLER

First published in 2012

The History Press
The Mill, Brimscombe Port
Stroud, Gloucestershire, GL5 2QG
www.thehistorypress.co.uk

British Library Cataloguing in Publication Data.
A catalogue record for this book is available from the British Library.

ISBN 978 0 7524 6527 2

Typesetting and origination by The History Press
Printed in India.

CONTENTS

ACKNOWLEDGEMENTS

We would like to thank the following for their insight into the history of particular buildings, and for allowing us access to take photographs: Chloe Green, Francesco Gitto (Jamie's Italian); Philip Jones (Horsley's Estate Agents); Gary Newman (Town Hall, Pittville Pump Room); The New Club; Paul Scott (The Playhouse); Mark and Fiona Stephens, Katy Garrity (the Daffodil); David and Robert Stevens, Sharon Walters (Paragon Laundry); Thai Brasserie, Carolyn Wood, and Justin Young (Queen's Hotel).

Our particular thanks to Michelle Tilling and Richard Leatherdale (The History Press), Denise Cain-Jones, for her specialist photographic skills, Fiona Needham and Molly Walker for their trusty proof-reading, and Darrel Kirby, author of *Gloucester Then & Now* (2012), for suggesting that we should write the book in the first place.

We would also like to thank all those who kindly gave permission for us to reproduce the following images: A.E. Bennett (www.transporttreasury.co.uk), p. 64; Denise Cain-Jones, pp. 32, 55, 60; Vic Cole, p. 69; Mavis Evans, p. 80; GCHQ, pp. 94, 95; *Gloucestershire Echo*, p. 13; Pam Herron, p. 50; Terry Langhorn, p. 89; Dave Martin, p. 91; Spencer McPherson, p. 20; Geoff and Elaine North, pp. 78, 90 and Kilian O'Sullivan (www.kilianosullivan.co.uk), pp. 22, 23. All other images are from the authors' collections.

Lastly we would like to thank our families and friends for their support and encouragement whenever we take on a new venture.

Our sources include: Gillian Avery, *Cheltenham Ladies* (2003); Michael Hasted, *A Theatre for All Seasons* (2011); James Hodsdon, *Historical Gazetteer of Cheltenham* (1997); Alan Moore, *Picture Palaces of Gloucester & Cheltenham* (undated); Neil Parrack, *The New Club at Imperial Square* (2011); Sue Rowbotham & Jill Waller, *Cheltenham, A History* (2004); Aylwin Sampson, *The Queen's Hotel* (1981); Peter Smith & Sue Rowbotham, *Commemorative Plaques of Cheltenham* (2009) and Ayako Yoshino, *Pageant Fever* (2011).

ABOUT THE AUTHORS

Sue Rowbotham and Jill Waller grew up in Cheltenham and met through their mutual interest in local history. They have researched a wide variety of lesser-known aspects of the town's past, and have published articles and books on Cheltenham, including *Cheltenham, A History* (2004). The performance of *Our Town Story: Cheltenham* at the Millenium Dome in 1999 was largely based on their research. In 2006 Sue and Jill were awarded a Cheltenham Arts Council citation for their ongoing services to local history.

The authors are keen to encourage others to uncover more of Cheltenham's history and to share this knowledge. Sue was editor of the Cheltenham Local History Society *Journal* from 2002 to 2008, and co-authored *Commemorative Plaques of Cheltenham* (2009) with the late Peter Smith. Jill has produced a series of themed chronologies of Cheltenham, providing a concise resource for other researchers.

INTRODUCTION

O ur challenge in compiling this book has been to include parts of the town not covered by previous publications. Where we have included well-known buildings, such as the Pump Rooms or the Town Hall, we have revealed less familiar facts. The Daffodil cinema and the County Court are classic examples of the changes of use that ensure the survival of some of Cheltenham's iconic buildings. Our original research has uncovered, for example, the history of the Montpellier Proscenium, and a study of the Food Reform Café shows that a fascination with healthy diets and celebrity endorsement is not a recent phenomenon. The all-pervasive smells of brewing from Whitbread's have long gone, but small independent breweries and retailers are becoming increasingly successful. We wonder what the Victorian gentlemen of 'approved rank' at the New Club would have made of the cupcakes and milkshakes now sold in Imperial Square.

Many of the early illustrations of Cheltenham are taken from our own collections. We have included coloured postcards reproducing paintings of the town, hand-coloured lithographs by well-known local artist George Rowe, engravings of events of national interest from the *Illustrated London News*, and even an original painting of the garage at Westal Green. Considerable artists' licence was used in early images of Cheltenham, usually to enhance the importance of particular buildings, as will be clear when comparing these images with the modern photographs.

Inevitably we can only give a glimpse of Cheltenham then and now, but hope to have highlighted how much the town has changed over the past 200 years, and how much has remained outwardly the same.

THE VIEW FROM LECKHAMPTON HILL

THE SAXONS ESTABLISHED CHELTENHAM about 1,200 years ago, on the River Chelt beside the Winchcombe to Gloucester road. Cheltenham is thought to mean a settlement (ham) under a hill or cliff (chilt), and has appeared as 'Chilteham', 'Chintenham' and 'Cheltham'. The earliest record of Cheltenham, dated AD 803, documents a dispute between the bishops of Worcester and Hereford over revenue from church lands there. Cheltenham's Manor next appeared in the 1086 Domesday Survey, when an administrative area roughly the size of the town's modern borough is estimated to have had a population of 114 male adults. In the 1540s Cheltenham was called 'Cheltenham Street' and described as 'a long town having a market', its layout reflecting its Saxon origins. Cheltenham's mineral waters, first exploited by Quaker William Mason in 1718, and developed by his son-in-law Henry Skillicorne, became fashionable following George III's visit in 1788. The town's expansion gathered momentum as new estates were developed in Pittville, Lansdown, Suffolk, Bayshill and The Park, particularly attracting retiring military officers and East India Company officials. There was also an influx of servants and tradesmen to support the town's wealthier inhabitants and visitors. By 1851 Cheltenham's population was 35,000. George Rowe's print shows, with considerable artistic licence, Cheltenham's most fashionable landmarks visible from Leckhampton Hill in 1840, including Christ Church and Pittville Pump Room.

IN THE TWENTIETH CENTURY, Cheltenham continued to flourish. New light industry was established in the area, including aerospace companies Dowty's and Smith's Industries, and large firms, such as Eagle Star and Kraft, moved their administrative headquarters here. Cheltenham's boundaries were extended to include Charlton Kings, Swindon Village, Up Hatherley, Leckhampton and Prestbury, and by 2001 the population was over 110,000. The modern photograph shows part of the extent of Cheltenham today. Both Christ Church tower and Eagle Tower give superb views over the town.

PARISH CHURCH
OF ST MARY

THE PARISH CHURCH OF ST MARY is Cheltenham's only remaining medieval building. It was built in the twelfth century by the Augustinian Cirencester Abbey, which supplied it with priests until the Dissolution of the Monasteries in 1539. The Crown then confiscated the rectory of Cheltenham, granting it to a succession of lessees including Sir Francis Bacon. Most of the church dates from the fourteenth century, including the magnificent circular rose window dedicated to St Katherine, seen here in this north-east view.

THE CHURCH UNDERWENT substantial renovations in 1859 and 1874, and the stained glass is Victorian. From 1729 to 1847 a small boys' charity school met in a room above the baptistry. Originally the schoolboys wore blue coats and yellow stockings that they had knitted themselves. In 1847 the school became the St Mary's Parish Boys' School and moved to Devonshire Street. The churchyard railings pictured opposite in 1898 have long gone. In May 1744 John Wesley preached from the fourteenth-century cross (having been barred from using the pulpit) and he recorded in his journal that the crowd 'seemed to understand just as much of the matter as if I had been talking Greek'. A tombstone of 1825 has the now legendary but barely legible inscription:

HERE LIES JOHN HIGGS,
A FAMOUS MAN FOR KILLING PIGS,
FOR KILLING PIGS WAS HIS DELIGHT
BOTH MORNING, AFTERNOON AND NIGHT.

BOTH HEATS AND COLD HE DID ENDURE,
WHICH NO PHYSICIAN COULD E'ER CURE;
HIS KNIFE IS LAID, HIS WORK IS DONE,
I HOPE TO HEAVEN HIS SOUL IS GONE.

Also in the churchyard are three small, brass measuring rods, set in the ground beside the path near the south-east corner of the church, which were used to measure lengths of rope and cloth when the market was nearby in the High Street. This peaceful heart of Cheltenham is now shaded by trees and populated by grey squirrels.

THE PLOUGH AND
THE REGENT ARCADE

A COACHING INN dating from at least 1654, the Plough was built when Cheltenham consisted of just one long street. In its heyday coaches departed from the Plough daily for London, the journey taking up to two days in the 1820s. The Plough yard, with its stables for 100 horses, carriage houses and granaries, was one of the largest in the country. The Royal Gloucestershire Hussars used the Plough as their headquarters from 1852 to 1893. Famous guests included violinist Niccolò Paganini, who was mobbed here in July 1831 by an angry crowd after refusing to play following a disagreement over his fee. For a different type of music, some may remember Granny's Folk Club at the Plough in the 1970s.

BETWEEN 1982 AND 1984 the Regent Arcade, designed by Dyer Associates, was built over the entire Plough site and beyond. Lost to the development were the old Town Hall (formerly a Baptist Chapel and a riding school, latterly a storeroom for Cavendish House), and the Regent Motors Garage where Frank Whittle assembled Britain's first jet engine in 1940–1. A small brass model of this jet is on display in the Arcade commemorating his achievement. Officially opened by Princess Anne in May 1985, the £23 million development provides 185,000 sq ft of floor space, 78 shops and parking for 540 cars.

THE 45ft, 3-ton WISHING FISH CLOCK was unveiled in January 1987, probably the world's tallest mechanical clock. Designed by author/artist Kit Williams and built by Michael Harding, it features a large, wooden fish, which wiggles its tail and blows bubbles to music every half hour. The Regent Arcade also displays a Victorian mosaic of a plough team, rescued from the entrance to the old Plough, and a royal coat of arms from the old Town Hall. The front of the Regent Arcade is currently (2012) being redesigned to provide space for a large clothing store.

THE ROYAL HOTEL AND BEECHWOOD SHOPPING CENTRE

THE ROYAL HOTEL opened in the early nineteenth century, a bustling coaching inn with an extensive livery yard that extended all the way through to Albion Street. An 1818 advertisement offered coaches daily to places as far afield as London, Exeter, Manchester and Liverpool. The coaching business declined with the arrival of the railways from the 1840s and, needing to diversify, the Royal Hotel's livery yard provided stabling for circus horses from 1856. In that year a permanent circus building was established in Bath Road, opening as Ryan's Equestrian Theatre in the grounds of Wellington Mansion, now the site of the Salvation Army Citadel. The theatre specialised in breathtaking displays of horsemanship and acrobatics. The flimsy building burned down in 1874 but was replaced by another on the same site. Also known as Ginnett's Hippodrome, and as the Colosseum, it was taken over by the Salvation Army in the 1880s and circuses no longer wintered in the town centre. An echo of the past occurred in the Beechwood Shopping Centre in April 2012, when Ukrainian acrobats from the Gloucestershire-based Gifford's Circus gave a performance as a publicity stunt.

A LARGE BRANCH OF WOOLWORTHS replaced the Royal Hotel after the Second World War, extending over the neighbouring property which appears today as a couple of set-back shops. This land was the original site of Pate's Almshouse, bought by Thomas Smith in 1811 for £250. The inmates were moved to the current, much smaller site in Albion Street and Smith resold the property for £2,000. The Vittoria Hotel was built on the site and the indented frontage of the present shops reflects its large front garden. The Vittoria was replaced in turn by Liverpool Place and then the £35 million Beechwood Shopping Centre opened on the site of the Royal and Vittoria Hotels in March 1991; it was sold on four years later for only £15 million.

THE ASSEMBLY ROOMS
AND LLOYDS BANK

NEW ASSEMBLY ROOMS were built on the High Street between 1815 and 1816 by Mr J.D. Kelly. 1,400 people attended the opening by the Duke and Duchess of Wellington on 29 July 1816 during one of their visits to Cheltenham, just a year after the Battle of Waterloo. The early print shows Williams' Library, which stood on the corner of the High Street and Rodney Road, and the distinctive porch and street lamps of the Assembly Rooms on the right.

The Assembly Rooms vied with Montpellier Spa for popularity and for the privileged there were weekly subscription balls, concerts and other entertainment in the imposing 87ft-long ballroom lit by eleven chandeliers in 'the season' between November and Easter. However, the rules stated categorically that 'no person hired or otherwise, in this town or neighbourhood; no person concerned in retail trade; no theatrical or other performer by profession, be permitted.'

MANY OF THE BEST-KNOWN MUSICIANS of the nineteenth century from Europe performed at the Assembly Rooms, including Strauss, Liszt, Paganini, Paderewski and the English contralto Clara Butt. Cheltenham-born 'Royal illusionists and anti-spiritualists' John Nevil Maskelyne and George Alfred Cooke performed at the Assembly Rooms on several occasions, as did many other conjurers, including Frenchman Jean Eugène Robert-Houdin, widely acclaimed as the 'Father of Modern Conjuring'. The last concert at the Assembly Rooms was given by the New Philharmonic Society on 16 May 1900, who performed worthy pieces by Schubert, Beethoven and Wagner.

Lloyds Bank demolished the Assembly Rooms, purchased in 1900, despite much opposition from those concerned about the loss of such a significant entertainment venue to the town. The new bank, designed by F.W. Waller and Son of Gloucester in the classical Baroque style, was opened in 1903.

THE BREWERY

BREWING WAS ONE of Cheltenham's earliest industries, and in 1712 the town was described as 'considerably engaged in malting'. Gardner's Brewery was founded in Fleece Lane (now Henrietta Street) in 1760 and it was an ideal site for brewing, with a 35ft deep well yielding 27,000 gallons of water daily. The Cheltenham Original Brewery, as it became known, gradually absorbed its smaller rivals in the town. The earlier picture shows the Brewery in 1898, extensively rebuilt with concrete arching, fireproof floors and wrought iron roof structures to a design by Messrs William Bradford & Sons, brewery architects of London, after a devastating fire in 1897.

Cheltenham's brewery continued to expand, taking over or amalgamating with other companies until it was acquired by Whitbread in 1963, becoming Whitbread Flowers in 1968. The brewery's administrative headquarters moved into the seven-storey Whitbread Tower in Monson Avenue, since demolished. Unfortunately, cask ale sales declined in the 1990s and the last beer was brewed on this site in 1998. However, a number of small independent breweries have recently begun operating in Cheltenham, including the Battledown, Festival and Prescott breweries. In 2012 Favourite Beers of Hewlett Road, with stocks including over 400 UK bottled ales, was awarded the national title of Independent Beer Retailer of the Year.

THE BREWERY OPENED in May 2006, after the site had lain derelict for several years. The attractive central tower of the Original Brewery survived demolition, and two red-brick walls from the four-storey malthouse on the corner of St Margaret's Road and Henrietta Street now form part of the façade for the new development. Today the Brewery houses an 11-screen multiplex cinema, gym and a number of restaurants and bars. A proposed £20 million scheme, announced in 2012, includes demolition of the 1960s High Street shops between Bennington Street and Henrietta Street, and construction of a new pedestrian link from the High Street to The Brewery.

CLARENCE STREET SHOPS

THE FOOD REFORM CAFÉ AND HEALTH FOOD STORES, which opened at No. 2 Clarence Street in 1927, promoted a wide variety of health foods, including finest quality dried fruits, shelled nuts, pure olive oil, grape wines, herbal remedies, home-made cakes and jams, wholemeal breads and 'wholegrain foods rich in vitamins'. The café boasted a number of brands, including Granose, who still manufacture a wide variety of meat-free meal mixes, and Ryvita and Vita-Weat biscuits, both of which are still produced today. They were also agents for products endorsed by British real tennis player Eustace Miles, silver medallist at the 1908 London Olympic Games, and prolific writer of books on health and diet.

CULT CLOTHING WAS FOUNDED in 1985 when Julian Dunkerton and a business partner began trading in second-hand jeans and T-shirts on an indoor market stall in Cheltenham, with money borrowed from Dunkerton's mother. The Cult Clothing designs, which combined vintage American fabrics with pseudo-Japanese text, proved very popular and the company was soon opening stores across the country, many in university towns and cities. In 2003 Julian Dunkerton was joined by designer James Holder to create a new in-house brand of clothing, named Superdry, which rapidly gained recognition and popularity both in the UK and overseas. Unusually, Superdry do not advertise or use celebrity endorsement, but the popularity of the brand grew rapidly after David Beckham was seen wearing one of the company's T-shirts. A second line of stores was opened, and further brands were launched for the skate and surf markets. The combined business, known as Supergroup, was floated very successfully on the London Stock Exchange in March 2010. Julian Dunkerton still lives in the Cheltenham area, and Cult Clothing, which is run from an industrial estate outside Cheltenham, now sells its products in over 300 countries across the world. The company's Cheltenham store is at No. 1 Clarence Street.

EVERYMAN THEATRE

CHELTENHAM'S FIRST THEATRE was a converted malt house and stables in Coffee House Yard, Pittville Street. There audiences saw some of the most famous actors of the day, including Sarah Siddons and her brother John Kemble. George III and his entourage attended the theatre three times during their visit to Cheltenham in 1788, allowing the venue to be renamed the Theatre Royal. A new Theatre Royal was built between Bath Street and the High Street in 1805, with supporters including Lord Byron. Sarah Siddons gave her final public performance, as Lady Macbeth, at the theatre in 1812, before retiring to live with her brother in North Street.

Disastrously, fire destroyed the Theatre Royal in 1839. The Revd Francis Close objected vehemently to all dramatic performances and, although plays were performed elsewhere in the town, Cheltenham did not have another theatre until well-known theatre architect Frank Matcham designed the Cheltenham Theatre and Opera House. This was opened in Regent Street on 1 October 1891 by Lillie Langtry in *Lady Clancarty* by Tom Taylor, with her own company from London's Princess Theatre.

THE THEATRE FLOURISHED until after the Second World War with many of the best-known theatre companies, opera companies and actors performing there, including D'Oyly Carte, Laurence Olivier and Charlie Chaplin. The increased popularity of television threatened closure in 1959, but following a public outcry the theatre was refurbished, and reopened as the Everyman in 1960 with a new repertory company.

A £3.2 million restoration of the Everyman took place in 2011, with the work carried out by local craftsmen. The theatre reopened on 2 October 2011 with *The Madness of King George* by Alan Bennett, to coincide with the 120th anniversary of the building. The Everyman Studio also revived *Lady Clancarty*, adapted in a new musical form by Paul Milton. The recent photograph shows the reopening celebrations in Regent Street.

COUNTY COURT
AND JAMIE'S ITALIAN

THE COUNTY COURT at the corner of Regent Street and County Court Road was built between 1869 and 1871 as the local civil court for the recovery of small debts. It was designed in the Italian renaissance style by the national Surveyor of County Courts, Thomas Charles Sorby, and built by the local firm of E. Billings & Son, using Postlip stone ashlar over brick. The carving and plasterwork were by Messrs Mabey, and the railings, topped by several fine lions, were made by Marshall's of Cheltenham. The interior includes fine red deal panelling, oak carvings and a roof lantern surrounded by ornate plaster mouldings.

The building is considered to be the only remaining example of a purpose-built county court in England. Opened on 6 January 1871, the judge on that first day was Charles Sumner Esq. The *Cheltenham Looker-On* reported that the 'peculiarly substantial and commodious' County Court was 'the first public building, properly so called, erected in Cheltenham'; all previous public buildings had been adaptations. Unusually, the courtroom has remained virtually unaltered, having never been partitioned into smaller units. The Cheltenham County Court closed in July 2005 and the Gloucestershire Courts Service moved

to the Magistrates' Court in St George's Road. The building needed major restoration as it suffered from damp, and the plumbing and electrical systems needed replacing.

ON 27 JULY 2011 the building was reopened as one of TV chef Jamie Oliver's restaurants, Jamie's Italian, providing rustic Mediterranean fare. Many of the original features have been retained in the conversion, and diners are able to eat while seated on the original bench or in the press box. Even the brick-lined cellar and underground cells are included in the scheme, in use as toilets and for storage. The County Court building is now a vibrant family restaurant employing approximately 90 people and the fine interior is now available for all to appreciate.

THE PROMENADE

GEORGE ROWE'S LITHOGRAPH of the Promenade dates
from about 1839. The Promenade was laid out in 1818
across former brickfields as a tree-lined drive leading to
the Sherborne Spa, now the site of the Queen's Hotel.
Development of residential villas and terraces followed from
the 1820s, although all these premises have gradually been
converted to commercial use. The balconied property on the
left was Wight's Theological Library in Rowe's time and is
now a branch of Jones, the boot and shoemakers, although
replica ornamental urns still grace the roof. Beyond this is
Cavendish House, Cheltenham's oldest department store.
It was opened at No. 3 Promenade Villas on 8 July 1826
by Thomas Clark and William Debenham of Wigmore
Street, near Cavendish Square in London. It expanded into
the neighbouring properties in the 1840s and '50s, and
for a time a large number of staff lived on the premises.
The business continued to expand under several changes
of ownership and in the 1960s underwent a complete
modernisation at a cost of £800,000, with the installation
of the façade we see today.

THE JEWELLER IN THE RIGHT FOREGROUND, Martin & Co., is one of Cheltenham's oldest businesses, established in the town by Samuel Martin in 1822. Martin's supplied the first Cheltenham Gold Cup of 1823 and has held the permanent contract to supply the Gold Cup, with other racing trophies, since 1933. The tall mid-terrace building on the right in Rowe's lithograph, probably designed by G.A. Underwood, was first occupied in 1823 by portrait painter Hamlet Millet. It later became the Imperial Hotel, then the exclusive gentlemen's Imperial Club, and from 1876 to 1987 it was Cheltenham's main post office.

It is currently a Waterstones bookshop. The railings and private gardens outside this terrace were removed in 1906. The vista to the Queen's Hotel is now obscured by trees planted during the pedestrianisation of the Promenade outside Cavendish House, providing shelter for a flourishing pavement café society.

LONG GARDEN, PROMENADE

THE LONG GARDEN ON THE PROMENADE was originally a railed private garden for residents of Harward's Buildings, the terrace on the right designed by G.A. Underwood in 1823. The central residences were converted for use as municipal offices between 1914 and 1916, and by 1958 the council occupied thirteen of the nineteen houses. The original Sherborne Spa Pump Room was re-sited at the far end of this terrace when the Queen's Hotel was built in 1837. It was replaced by the Regal, later ABC cinema, which opened in January 1939. This closed in 1981 to be replaced by an office building.

IN THE FOREGROUND IS THE BOER WAR MEMORIAL, a figure of a soldier unveiled on 17 July 1907 by General Sir Ian Hamilton. It stands on a plinth that bears the names of all Cheltenham men who served in the Boer War, including those who died. In the centre is the war memorial, unveiled on 21 October 1921. The simple 24ft cenotaph by R.L. Boulton & Sons is engraved with the names of Cheltenham men who gave their lives in both world wars. Beyond this is a memorial to Cheltenham-born Edward Adrian Wilson, who served as Chief of Scientific Staff on the 1910–13 Antarctic *Terra Nova* expedition. He was one of the five men who reached the South Pole in January 1912, but who perished shortly afterwards. The statue, modelled by leader Captain Scott's widow, was unveiled on 11 July 1914. To commemorate the 100th anniversary of that expedition the Wilson Memorial Statue was rededicated, and three new information plaques unveiled, on 18 March 2012. The modern photograph shows the farmers' market, a regular part of Promenade life on the second and last Fridays of each month. The roadworks in the foreground mark the original cobbled road surface, uncovered and relaid in early 2012.

THE NEW CLUB AND
THE QUADRANGLE

THE NEW CLUB opened as a private gentlemen's club on 31 October 1874 on the corner of the Promenade and Imperial Square, replacing the Gloucestershire and Cheltenham Club which had been located above the Assembly Rooms (now Lloyds Bank) in the High Street. Access to the New Club was restricted to 'visitors of approved rank in society', almost exclusively prominent citizens and the higher ranks of the armed services. In 1970 the New Club moved a short distance to new premises at No. 2 Montpellier Parade, a much more attractive Regency building in a quieter location which had previously been a private house and a school. Today the New Club is described as a 'private members' club for men and women of the professional and business community', offering members a wide range of facilities and events, including lunches, dinners and private functions, a marquee at Cheltenham Cricket Festival and two boxes at the Cheltenham racecourse.

THE QUADRANGLE, a bland multi-storey concrete and glass office block built for Gulf Oil in 1973, replaced the old New Club on Imperial Square. Fortunately, part of the original decorative cast iron canopy from the New Club doorway can still be seen at Belgrave House (now Pizza Express) opposite, and many of the original furnishings and fittings from the club were transferred to Montpellier Parade, including the full-sized snooker table, the high-backed and enclosed leather porter's chair, which still stands by the front door, and the brass name plate. The Quadrangle, which has been described as an 'offensive, shabby and indefensible' eyesore on the Promenade, was given a boost when the independent family-run Swallow Bakery, which began in Chichester, opened its second outlet in Cheltenham in 2010, selling fashionable speciality cupcakes, cakes and dessert pies made on the premises.

THE WINTER GARDENS
AND FESTIVALS

THE WINTER GARDENS opened in Imperial Square in 1878 and soon became one of Cheltenham's prime venues for a wide variety of popular entertainments, particularly for those unable to enjoy the pleasures of the Assembly Rooms. Designed by J.T. Darby, the Winter Gardens were constructed by the Central Iron Works in Lansdown and included one of the earliest roller skating rinks in the country and the Cinema de Luxe, 'the most luxurious picture palace in the west of England', which opened in 1912. The enormous building, flanked by gardens, tennis courts and a bowling green, stretched from the back of where the Town Hall stands today as far as the Queen's Hotel, but predated the Town Hall by some twenty-five years.

DESPITE ITS ATTRACTIONS, the Winter Gardens venue was far from ideal. The cast iron and glass construction made it difficult and expensive to maintain. It was cold in winter, and hot in summer, and Imperial Square residents could often hear concerts as clearly as those who had bought tickets.

The building was finally demolished between 1940 and 1943, supposedly because it was an easy target for German bombers. A more likely explanation was that the council were glad of an excuse to be rid of it. Remnants of the Winter Gardens are still visible in Imperial Gardens, including the chequered brickwork base of one of the towers.

Imperial Gardens and the site of the Winter Gardens still play an important part in Cheltenham's entertainment throughout the year. Marquees are set up as venues for talks, concerts and hospitality particularly during the town's many festivals. These include the Music Festival (first held just three weeks after the end of the Second World War), the Literature Festival (launched by Cheltenham-born actor Ralph Richardson in 1949), the International Jazz Festival, the Folk Festival and the Science Festival. The year 2012 saw the introduction of a Spring Fashion Festival.

THE TOWN HALL

CHELTENHAM NEEDED A NEW ENTERTAINMENT VENUE with the closure of the Assembly Rooms in 1900. The Winter Gardens were not considered an 'acceptable permanent substitute', so it was agreed that much larger Municipal Assembly Rooms should be built on the Winter Gardens bowling green in Imperial Square. A memorial stone, with a bottle containing local newspapers and coinage of the day, was laid at the site on 1 October 1902 to commemorate the coronation of Edward VII and Queen Alexandra. The new Town Hall, as it was soon renamed, was built by Collins & Godfrey of Tewkesbury to a design by F.W. Waller at a cost of £45,000. Not everyone admired the ornate interior, and one critic described the dark red marble columns and gold Corinthian capitals in the Grand Main Hall as 'corned beef topped with mustard'.

THE FIRST CONCERT AT THE TOWN HALL was performed by the 70-piece Cheltenham Philharmonic Society, conducted by C.J. Phillips on 28 January 1904. In 1906 the borough council began promoting Cheltenham extensively as a spa town and the new Central Spa was opened in the Town Hall, with women in frilled aprons and caps dispensing water from the Montpellier and Pittville Spas. The earlier photograph, above right, shows a typical morning scene at the Central Spa Lounge in 1922. Today this room, shown here laid out for a conference, is known as the Dining Room.

Comedian Norman Wisdom, billeted at the Moray Hotel (now Hotel du Vin), was encouraged by actor Rex Harrison to become an entertainer following a charity concert at the Town Hall during the Second World War, and many up-and-coming comedians have played there since, including Michael McIntyre and Tim Minchin. Today Cheltenham Town Hall is the hub of the town's many festivals, and a popular venue for shows, conferences and other events. In 2012 the first wedding was performed in the building.

IMPERIAL GARDENS

THE ORNATE, PAGODA-SHAPED BANDSTAND was unveiled in the Imperial Gardens outside the Winter Gardens building on 3 May 1920. Costing an impressive £1,850, the bandstand was cast at Walter Macfarlane & Co.'s Saracen Foundry in Glasgow for Cheltenham Borough Council. The bandstand is still in use, but was sold to Bognor Regis in 1948 for a mere £175. For many years the site of the bandstand was an ornamental pond and fountain.

ON 4 APRIL 2008 a statue of the composer Gustav Holst was unveiled on the site. Holst was born at No. 4 Clarence Road in Cheltenham in 1874 and attended Pate's Grammar School where his father, Adolph Holst, taught music. Gustav also showed an early aptitude for music and in 1892 he composed an operetta entitled *Lansdown Castle*, named after a crenellated building at the junction of Lansdown Road and Gloucester Road. The piece was enthusiastically received when first performed at Cheltenham Corn Exchange the following year, and Adolph was sufficiently impressed to borrow money to send his son to the Royal College of Music in London. Holst returned to Cheltenham in the late 1920s and remained here until his death in 1934.

THE GUSTAV HOLST MEMORIAL FOUNTAIN statue was created by sculptor Anthony Stones and cast at the Pangolin Foundry in Chalford. Observant onlookers will notice that the composer is holding his baton in his left hand – he often had to conduct left-handed as he suffered severe neuritis in his right hand. The same foundry also cast seven plaques, incorporated in the octagonal plinth, which depict the planets after Holst's best-known work *The Planets*. The memorial, costing more than £50,000, was largely paid for with a legacy left to the Civic Society by Miss Elizabeth Hamond. At the unveiling the Pate's Grammar School orchestra played 'Fanfare to Gustav Holst', especially composed by Holst scholar Raymond Head for the event.

THE QUEEN'S HOTEL

THE NEO-CLASSICAL QUEEN'S HOTEL, designed by R.W. & C. Jearrad, was built in 1837–8 at the top of the Promenade at a cost of £47,000. It was built on the site of the Sherborne Spa, which had to be carefully dismantled and moved further down the Promenade, to where Royscot House is now, behind the Neptune fountain. The elegant glass porch and two electric lamps surmounted by gilded crowns were removed in 1905. The first lessee was Richard Liddell, who paid £2,100 to take on more than 120 bedrooms, 30 sleeping apartments for servants, 25 sitting rooms, as well as drawing rooms, a billiard room, a ballroom and a coffee room. In 1852 the hotel was sold to W.S. Davis for £8,400. Two Russian guns were once displayed outside the hotel, captured at the siege of Sebastopol and given to Cheltenham in 1856 by the then Secretary of State for War, Lord Panmure. The proprietor, Mr Davis, allowed the guns to be stored in the hotel stables and also defrayed the cost of mounting them on their cast iron plinths. The mounted guns were officially unveiled on 5 July 1858. Only one plinth remains and it bears the names of Crimean War casualties. The cannon were removed along with many of the town's railings in the Second World War scrap metal drive.

IMPROVEMENTS AND ALTERATIONS have been made continually and in about 1900 even a darkroom was provided for guests who might be amateur photographers. During the Second World War the Queen's was used as an American Services Club. To the east of the Queen's lay the hotel's stableyard, which could accommodate 70 horses with their carriages. There was also a smithy and a brewery on the site. This area became a garage in 1925 as the motorcar became the favoured means of transport, and in 1995 a neo-Regency residential terrace was built here.

NAPOLEON FOUNTAIN
AND JUBILEE SEAT

SUPPOSEDLY THIS FOUNTAIN was the work of late eighteenth-century Genoan sculptor Bruni, looted by Napoleon's army in Italy and then captured at sea on its way to France by an English privateer. In 1826 it was bought by Cheltenham solicitor Thomas Henney, who installed it in a pavilion near his Sherborne or Imperial Spa (now the site of the Queen's Hotel). Originally operated by a steam engine, the fountain reportedly sent jets of water 32ft into the air. In 1834 the Napoleon Fountain was moved to Montpellier Gardens, as seen in the print. The Chinese pagoda in the background was erected in 1831 by the Jearrad brothers, lessees of the Montpellier and Imperial Spas. The flag beyond the trees is on the roof of the Montpellier Rotunda. After being re-sited nearer the Rotunda, the fountain languished in Montpellier Gardens until 1902. After restoration it was displayed in the Town Hall lobby from 1906 until 1925, then in the Public Library foyer until 1964, when it was put into storage at the museum. It could be seen at Lloyds Bank, Montpellier, for some years from 1986. The fountain is now housed at the end of the 1995 neo-Regency terrace, the Broad Walk, near its original location overlooking Imperial Gardens.

IN MONTPELLIER GARDENS TODAY, near where the Napoleon Fountain was situated, is the Jubilee seat, commissioned by the Cheltenham Arts Council to commemorate Queen Elizabeth II's Golden Jubilee. Costing £12,000, it was designed by the Stroud sculptor David John. The five sides of the seat mark the decades of the Queen's reign and the encircling musical notes represent the first lines of the national anthem. During the unveiling in May 2003 a flock of 15 racing pigeons was released, an appropriate gesture as pigeons are credited with drawing attention to the first mineral spring on Bayshill. Cheltenham is also home to the Royal Pigeon Racing Association headquarters.

MONTPELLIER GARDENS AND THE PROSCENIUM

MONTPELLIER GARDENS were laid out in 1831 as pleasure grounds for the Montpellier Spa, and have always been a popular location for public entertainment. The Victorian bandstand in Montpellier Gardens was constructed in 1864 to a design by the Coalbrookdale Company, Ironbridge, and is believed to be the oldest bandstand in the country still in regular use. The distinctive Elizabethan-style proscenium was constructed in 1900 by a Mr Yeates for £322, who had also tendered for the two wooden bandstands in Pittville Park. The proscenium, which had dressing rooms in the towers at either side of the stage, provided the backdrop for entertainments, such as the summer concerts, which were becoming increasingly popular. The first performances on the stage were by Mr Henry Beaumont's Opera Company, from Covent Garden, and the Carl Rosa Opera Company on 19 July 1900.

THE AWNING THAT EXTENDS from the proscenium towards the bandstand in the earlier photograph provided shelter for an audience facing in either direction. This temporary structure was replaced by a permanent building in about 1911, known as the Montpellier Pavilion, and later simply as the Pavilion. The Pavilion was used as a clubhouse for the very successful Cheltenham Table Tennis Club and Cheltenham Gymnastics Club. Many people may remember the Pavilion Club in the 1970s, which hosted discos, such as the Split Six, and many live bands, including Ravenstone, Guilty But Insane and Gentle Edge. The Pavilion is thought to have been demolished in the late 1970s.

A green plaque on the bandstand commemorates the refurbishment of Montpellier Gardens on 9 July 2007, funded by £722,000 from the Heritage Lottery. Many of the 1923 features of the gardens were restored, including the proscenium, which now houses the Gardens Gallery, a community gallery for local artists. Montpellier Gardens are still a thriving location for entertainment, including the Cheltenham Food and Drink Festival, and even a temporary ice-skating rink.

MONTPELLIER ROTUNDA

IN MARCH 1808 Henry Thompson, a banker who played a large part in developing nineteenth-century Cheltenham, opened the first Montpellier Spa, erecting a wooden Long Room over the pump the following year. Water from over 80 saline wells on his land was pumped to the spa. George Allen Underwood, a former assistant to renowned London architect Sir John Soane, replaced the wooden building with a more permanent structure in 1817, adding the plain Doric colonnade that still fronts Montpellier Walk. In 1824 Henry's son Pearson Thompson continued development of Montpellier and Lansdown. His architect John Buonarotti Papworth designed the 160ft diameter, 60ft high domed Rotunda that was erected over the spa in 1825–6. The interior was originally lined with mirrors and the corridors bore murals of hunting scenes. Behind the stone lion above the entrance, and curiously out of sight from the ground, is the carved motto *Infirmo capiti fluit utilis utilis alvo* – 'Our waters cure head and stomach complaints'. The Duke of Wellington visited Montpellier Spa and endorsed its curative powers in alleviating his liver complaint. Horticultural exhibitions, balls and concerts were held here, including a performance by Jenny Lind in 1848.

THE LONG ROOM originally housed a reading room, a billiard room and a 'boiling room' for those who favoured the more strongly purgative effects of heated spa water. The Long Room was taken over by the Worcester City & County Bank in 1882. In 1889 this bank was absorbed by Lloyds Bank, who shared the premises with other commercial enterprises including Frederick Wright Ltd, tobacco merchant. In the 1950s and '60s the Rotunda was home to a popular Dancing School run by Mrs Annette Stammers, assisted by Lady Colwyn. Lloyds Bank bought the Rotunda in 1961 for £14,000 and carried out a major renovation; it now occupies the whole of Montpellier Spa, using the Rotunda as a banking hall.

MONTPELLIER EXCHANGE

MAWE AND TATLOW'S MUSEUM in Montpellier was opened by John Mawe and his son-in-law Anthony Tissington Tatlow in 1816. Derby-born Mawe, one-time sailor and stonemason, became a dealer and acknowledged expert in mineralogy and diamond-cutting, and collected minerals and shells around the world. He set up in business in London, and by 1804 he claimed that collectors would 'find the largest Variety of Minerals and Shells in Europe' at his Covent Garden shop. His best-selling account of being the first European permitted to visit Brazil's mineral treasures, *Travels in the Interior of Brazil* (1812), was carried by Charles Darwin aboard the *Beagle* in the 1830s. In 1812 John Mawe opened a new shop at 149 Strand, London, and from here he published erudite books, often beautifully illustrated in colour, which are still highly prized. Mawe continued trading until his death in 1829, having helped establish commercial mineralogy in Britain. His wife Sarah carried on the business, and had the title 'Mineralogist to Her Majesty' until she retired in 1840.

THE MONTPELLIER EXCHANGE, which replaced Mawe
and Tatlow's in 1843, originally comprised three shops,
and may have been designed by S.W. Daukes and
J. Hamilton who were also responsible for shops in Rotunda
Terrace and Montpellier Street. A typical business for
the area was Parisian milliner and dressmaker Madame
Begnault, who moved from 104 High Street to
1 Montpellier Exchange in January 1845. The marble
statue in front of the Exchange is inscribed 'ER 1914.
In memory of HM King Edward VII the Peacemaker' and
depicts the king informally dressed and holding the hand
of a little girl. The statue, designed by Ambrose Neale, and
produced by R.L. Boulton, Cheltenham, was donated by
Mr and Mrs Drew of Hatherley Court, who were
well-known for rescuing old horses and donkeys.
The marble plinth includes a horse trough, a dog trough
and three lion's head drinking fountains.

MONTPELLIER WINE BAR

THE BOW-FRONTED BUILDING at the top of the west side of Montpellier Street, formerly
No. 1 Rotunda Terrace, existed by 1851, initially home to H. Collett, paperhanger. From the
1890s to the 1920s the property was called Bayshill Lodge, and from 1896 it was home to
a chemist, Philip Thomas. His family had opened a shop further down the terrace in 1894.
Their shop reopened at Bayshill Lodge and became the Spa Pharmacy, as seen in the earlier
photograph. The firm had another branch, the College Pharmacy at the corner of St Luke's Road
and Bath Road. The Spa Pharmacy advertised that it was the Cheltenham depot for all surgical
appliances, and claimed to be the best supplier of all photographic equipment and supplies. In
1911 the firm merged with another chemist on the opposite corner of Montpellier Street and
relocated there as Thomas, Saxby & Milne Ltd.

BAYSHILL LODGE OPENED IN 1914 as the Spa Temperance Hotel with E.G. Jennings as proprietor.
During 1916–17 it was known as Jennings' Refreshment Room before closure in 1917. By 1924
the property had changed hands again and Frank George Fildes opened his grocery shop in the
building. Messrs Fildes & Beard had a grocery further down Montpellier Street at 6 Rotunda
Terrace from 1911. Fildes' grocery remained at the top of Montpellier Street throughout much of
the twentieth century, with the family living above the shop. Signs of the building's former use as
a grocery can be seen in the stained-glass frieze of fruit and vegetables that embellishes the top of
the ground-floor windows. The building was refitted as the Montpellier Wine Bar in the 1970s and
remains part of Montpellier's vibrant social scene. The modern photograph shows how café society
has taken a hold in Cheltenham, with chairs and tables placed on the pavement for customers to
enjoy their drinks outside.

THE GORDON LAMP

IN MARCH 1885 a memorial was proposed to Major-General Charles George Gordon, who had been killed during the defence of Khartoum earlier that year. By May, only £200 had been raised by subscription so the 'Gordon Lamp' was erected instead to embellish the area then known as the Montpellier Cross. The lamp, consisting of a fluted iron shaft topped by three glass bulbs and supported by three cherubs with torches mounted on a polished grey and red Scottish granite base, is described as 'an outstanding example of late nineteenth-century street furniture' and is Grade II listed by English Heritage. The gas lamp was first lit on 11 May 1887, despite much debate about the cost of running it, and was adapted for electricity in 1899–1900.

A commemorative tablet was finally added to the lamp's base by the Scottish Society in 1933.

GORDON BOYS' CLUBS sprang up across the country in the patriotic fervour that followed Major-General Gordon's death in 1885. Cheltenham's Gordon Boys' Brigade was set up in May 1890 with '20 lads', and was formally inaugurated on 28 May at the club's headquarters at 1 Liverpool Place (left of the entrance to the Beechwood Shopping Centre). The uniformed boys were available at various sites, including Montpellier, to run errands. The Cheltenham Brigade was in existence for at least sixteen years.

In 1871 Miss Elizabeth Baillie of Tivoli offered to erect a drinking fountain 'for the comfort of the poor and to the ornament of the town' on this site. However, the Town Commissioners were concerned about the cost of supplying the fountain with water, and the fact that it might become a 'serious nuisance'. Instead they proposed replacing a cab stand in Clarence Street with her fountain, but the resulting dispute with the cab drivers evidently exasperated Miss Baillie, who donated £110 to Cheltenham General Hospital instead.

WESTAL GREEN GARAGE

THE MOTORCAR HAD AN INCREASING IMPACT on Cheltenham from the 1890s. In March 1899 a Bristol motorist was fined for driving furiously in Pittville Street, and in June 1903 another was fined £2 for recklessly driving at 20mph in Bath Road. The first purpose-built filling station in Cheltenham was erected on part of Westal Green in 1928, despite protests from residents and town councillors, one describing it as a 'hideous thing coming into the town'. The proprietor Oliver Goulding had bought the land and the council were unable to refuse building approval, but Mr Goulding made every effort to ensure the pagoda-style petrol station would be acceptable to all. His architect was Clough Williams-Ellis, of Portmeirion fame, a founder member of the Council for the Protection of Rural England. Goulding had the support of at least one neighbour who wrote to the local press stating that the proposed shrubs and flowers screening the pumps would be much make more attractive than 'the three large, ragged, ill-kept, neglected trees which are allowed to block up the N.E. corner of the site in question'.

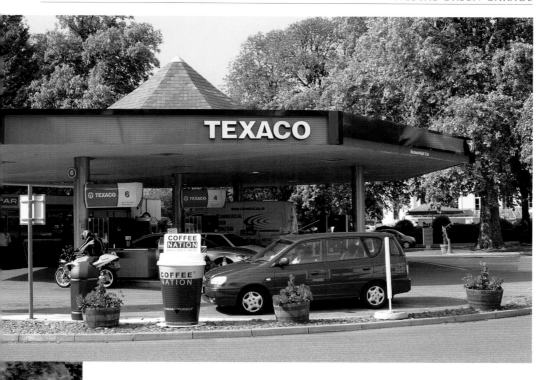

PROUD OF HIS NEW FILLING STATION, Mr Goulding entered it in the 1929 *Daily Express* Brighter Petrol Stations contest. He was awarded fourth place and presented with a silver cup by the Russian Oil Company. He also built himself a new house, which still overlooks the petrol station on the corner of Lansdown and Andover Roads, clearly not designed by Clough Williams-Ellis. Mrs Goulding sold fruit and flowers from an adjacent small shop. When petrol was only 1*s* 1½*d* per gallon customers included Tommy Walls of Wall's Ice Cream, archaeologist and Egyptologist Howard Carter, and the author of *Three Men in a Boat*, Jerome K. Jerome. The Williams-Ellis building was replaced in the 1970s but the present Texaco canopy reflects the original design. It was given a £170,000 refurbishment in 2010.

PARAGON LAUNDRY

THE FAMILY-RUN BUSINESS Paragon Laundry was established in 1918, as the company slogan states – 'Squeaky clean since 1918'. Initially horse-drawn carts collected and delivered the laundry, but the company soon started using motor vans. Paragon's first purpose-built laundry was established in Hatherley Road, echoing a familiar pattern in Cheltenham – as the town grew following the discovery of the spa water in 1716, washerwomen offered their services around the outskirts of the town in areas such as Alstone, Leckhampton and Hatherley, where they could provide extensive drying-grounds. Paragon's original business, offering domestic laundry services to private households, rapidly began to dwindle with the arrival of domestic washing machines. To counteract this the adaptable company targeted commercial concerns such as hospitals, hotels and factories, offering not just laundry services but also linen and workwear rental.

Paragon has always embraced the latest technology, thus retaining market leadership. However, it was not the first in Cheltenham to introduce innovations in the world of laundry. Robert William Jearrad, architect of much of the Montpellier and Lansdown estates, Christ Church and the Queen's Hotel, invented a washing machine in 1849. It was successfully trialled in the St George's Workhouse, Hanover Square, London, and proved excellent for sterilising the clothing of cholera victims. It was also economic, able to wash six dozen towels in just four minutes, suggesting it could be indispensable to 'hospitals, workhouses, ships, baths and wash-houses for the poor, and in private houses', providing a great saving in soap, time and labour.

FROM SMALL BEGINNINGS IN CHELTENHAM, Paragon has expanded to become one of the country's biggest independent commercial laundry companies. Recently business was extended to the Middle East with operations in Qatar and Dubai. There is still a laundry on the original site in Hatherley Road, but much of the original building complex has been replaced with state-of-the-art facilities.

MONTPELLIER BATHS
AND THE PLAYHOUSE

HENRY THOMPSON OPENED HIS MONTPELLIER BATHS in 1806, offering fourteen warm baths and one large cold bath, and established a Salts Manufactory on the site to which spa water was piped from over 70 wells sunk in Montpellier and Lansdown. Thompson's 'Real Cheltenham Salts' were sold nationwide, although business suffered when it was falsely suggested that Epsom salts were being added to the product. Henry's son, Pearson Thompson, expanded the baths and they were further improved by architects R.W. and C. Jearrad. A steam-driven corn mill and bakery were also part of the site, utilising the steam that was a by-product of salt extraction. The square brick chimney that rose from the boiler room was demolished in 1984.

FROM THE 1860s Cheltenham College held annual diving competitions at Montpellier Baths, until they acquired their own swimming bath in 1880. Annual public swimming matches were held from 1881 and water polo was played from the 1890s. Also, from 1881 the Montpellier Baths Company boarded over the pool for use as a gymnasium during winter months. A Gymnasium Club was set up which gave annual displays in March. The adaptation also provided a hall for meetings and dances.

Cheltenham Corporation bought Montpellier Baths in 1898, reopening it in September 1900 following extensive refurbishment that included fibrous plasterwork by H.H. Martyn. New medicinal bathing facilities were introduced, and treatments in the 1920s included 'Radio-Active Mud Baths' for rheumatoid arthritis. A 1910 town guide advertised the swimming pool for hire by private parties – 'any depth of water may be ordered, the water being fresh every time the bath is used'. In 1945 Cheltenham Borough Council converted Montpellier Baths into the Civic Playhouse Theatre for use by amateur drama companies. Now permanently covered beneath the auditorium, the white tiles lining the pool can still be seen under the stage. The Playhouse remains in regular use by local theatre groups.

RODNEY ROAD

IN THE 1960s a 'Trust The Motorist Car Park' opened at the southern end of Rodney Road, one of a series of methods used to regulate parking in Cheltenham. Ironically, despite the name, the payment boxes had firmly padlocked straps attached to deter thieves. In 1953 a proposal to introduce parking meters to the town was met with dismay by town councillors, with one declaring the idea of paying to park 'isn't cricket!' A free 'Disc-parking' system was in use in the 1960s, but 'Pay & Display' has been the favoured method of town centre parking management for several decades now. Recently a rash of 'Pay & Display' machines have sprung up in many residential areas too. Planning policies over the years have inadvertently ensured people are increasingly reliant on car use and so parking problems persist.

AN 1820 POST OFFICE MAP shows a very large circular pond on this site, probably part of the garden of nearby Cambray House. In 1834 the octagonal chalybeate Cambray Spa was built here at the junction with Oriel Road for Baynham Jones of Cambray House. In 1873 it became William Ruck's Turkish Bath, demolished in 1938. In the early twentieth century surgeon John Howell of Imperial Square adopted the rest of the site for use as a garden as his house did not have one. Across the road can be seen the ornate porch of The Woodlands. This brick-built villa is one of the earliest buildings in Rodney Road and is on a different alignment. It was built right beside the Chelt (now culverted) in 1813 by Charles Yeates, a gardener. A noticeable join in the brickwork shows where the property was increased in depth in the 1820s or '30s, the windows in the rear half being in quaint Regency Gothick. The Woodlands remained in private hands until 1969 when it became Horsley's estate agency.

EAGLE LODGE
AND EAGLE TOWER

THESE TWO BUILDINGS MIGHT SEEM WORLDS APART, but the Eagle Tower, Cheltenham's tallest building, and the demure Regency building, which stands in its shadow, share a fascinating history. Montpellier Lodge, at the junction of Montpellier Drive and Bath Road, was built as a private house in 1838. Montpellier Lodge was sold by its last private owner to the nearby Langton Hotel in the 1930s and renamed the Montpellier Hotel. Both establishments shared the same proprietor for a brief period. The last owner of the Montpellier Hotel was Mrs Meredith, the wife of F.W. Meredith, a well-known pioneer in flight control systems, who worked at Smith's Industries. The much larger Langton Hotel (see below), at 93–5 Bath Road, was also originally a private house. From the 1930s the Irving Hotel was a competitor, a few hundred yards away on the corner of Suffolk Road, at 105–7 Bath Road. It was owned by Mrs Irving, mother of Charles Irving, Cheltenham's MP from 1974 to 1992. 'An actress and extrovert with a passion for worthy causes', she had previously owned a dance studio at this address.

THE EAGLE STAR INSURANCE COMPANY bought the Montpellier Hotel in 1965, together with other properties on the extensive Bath Road site, including the Langton Hotel. In October 1968 Eagle Star moved from its prestigious location in Threadneedle Street, London, to a purpose-built head office on the new site, which included the controversial 13-storey Eagle Tower that was built where the Langton Hotel had once stood. Montpellier Lodge was renamed Eagle Lodge, and became a staff hostel, and later offices and a conference centre. In 1984 Eagle Star was acquired by BAT Industries for £968 million, and the brand is now owned by Zurich Financial Services, with offices in Bishop's Cleeve. In 2005 Eagle Lodge became the Spice Lodge restaurant, serving authentic Pan Asian cuisine, and was voted best curry house in the South-West at the British Curry Awards 2011.

THE DAFFODIL

THE DAFFODIL PICTURE HOUSE opened at 5.30 p.m. on 5 October 1922
at 16–17 Suffolk Parade, showing the silent movie *Thunderclap* starring
Mary Carr. The cinema was built in flamboyant Art Deco style with mosaic
daffodils in the floor of the foyer, and plaster daffodils decorating the walls
in the foyer and main auditorium. The Daffodil seated up to 750 people, and
boasted special 'courting seats', which could be reserved by telephone.
The developer, Fred Sims, a local baker and confectioner, was also a corn
and flour dealer, with premises accessed from the lane behind the cinema.
With the advent of 'talkies' a sophisticated sound system replaced the
original orchestral accompaniment at the Daffodil in 1930. During
the Second World War the single British Pathé newsreel provided for
Cheltenham had to be transported by bicycle between all six cinemas
in town. Falling attendance with the advent of television, increased
competition and vandalism eventually forced the closure of the Daffodil on
7 September 1963, with the thriller *Cape Fear* starring Gregory Peck and
Robert Mitchum being the last film shown. The building was run as a bingo
club until 1977 when it became a second-hand furniture salesroom. Sadly
neglected, the building fell into disrepair, with a leaking roof and damaged
plasterwork, and finally closed in 1989.

IN 1996 CHELTENHAM RESTAURATEUR Mark Stephens fell in love with the decaying building and purchased the freehold. On 14 February 1998 the Daffodil reopened as a restaurant, with many of the building's original Art Deco features lovingly restored. The original projectors are displayed in what was the Upper Circle, from which two curving staircases now sweep dramatically down to the dining area below. The present interior was designed by Laurence Llewelyn Bowen. In 2011 the Daffodil sponsored the newly-formed Cheltenham Film Festival and hosted several events, including a screening of the 1929 silent movie, *Piccadilly* with live piano accompaniment by Stephen Horne. This was the first film to be shown in the Daffodil since 1963.

SHAFTESBURY HALL
AND CHELSEA COURT

THE REVD FRANCIS CLOSE was instrumental in the development of Cheltenham as one of the earliest centres for teacher training. Established on strict 'Scriptural, Evangelical and Protestant principles' the Normal College opened in 1847 in two rented rooms with seven male students. Astonishingly, twelve women students joined the following year in what was considered a 'hazardous experiment'. After being housed at the former High Street Hospital (now Normandy House) and then at The Priory, London Road, the female department was moved to the purpose-built St Mary's Hall, St George's Place, in 1869. By 1886 the department was considered to be 'in some respects at the head of all the Female Training Colleges in the Kingdom', but it was not until 1908 that a Miss Armstrong became the first woman student to obtain a London BA degree through the college.

IN 1921 THE FEMALE DEPARTMENT became
St Mary's College of Education, a college in its own right,
and moved to The Park. St Paul's College of Education
took over St Mary's Hall, renaming it Shaftesbury Hall.
Many will remember the hall as the venue for music
concerts and discos in the 1970s and '80s.

The two colleges recombined to become the College of
St Paul's and St Mary's in 1979, and merged with the
Gloucestershire College of Art and Technology in 1990
to become Cheltenham and Gloucester College of Higher
Education. In 2001 the college became the University of
Gloucestershire, and today has three campuses; Francis
Close Hall, a landmark in the centre of Cheltenham for
nearly 200 years, The Park and Oxstalls, on the outskirts
of Gloucester. Shaftesbury Hall was granted Grade II
listed status in 1988, in recognition of its importance
as an early, specially designed building for women's
education. The building was converted into spacious
luxury apartments in 1998, and today forms part of the
development known collectively as Chelsea Court.

ST JAMES AREA

IN THE 1820s Charles Hale Jessop established his Nursery Gardens, with 20 acres of landscaped grounds, hothouses and greenhouses on the banks of the River Chelt. Entry to the gardens was free and visitors came to admire the exotic plants which grew there, such as rice, bananas and breadfruit. Disaster struck on 26 July 1855 when tons of debris were swept through the nursery by a raging torrent, submerging parts beneath 7ft of floodwater. The damage was estimated to have been 10 per cent of the entire cost to the town, and Jessop was declared bankrupt in 1858. The family continued to trade but the Nursery finally closed in 1872.

IN 1847 CHELTENHAM'S SECOND RAILWAY STATION was opened at the end of Knapp Lane, close to where St Gregory's Primary School stands today, on land bought from Jessop's Nursery. The broad gauge track between Cheltenham and Gloucester, originally built in 1840, then became the last stage of the Great Western Railway line, which ran from Cheltenham through Gloucester, Stonehouse, Stroud and Kemble, and terminated at Swindon. Much of the route is still in use today by commuters between Cheltenham and London Paddington. The track was converted to standard gauge in 1872, and a much larger station was built further north in 1894, with a massive covered portico facing St James' Square. By 1904 the station was handling large quantities of goods and passenger traffic. Sadly St James' station fell victim to the controversial Beeching cuts, and had closed to all traffic by October 1966. The extensive derelict site remained an eyesore until it was finally developed by the Waitrose supermarket chain in 2002. A green Cheltenham Civic Society plaque beside the store's entrance commemorates the station, and today's shoppers waiting at the checkouts are an echo of the many passengers who waited to board their trains here for more than 125 years.

ALPHA HOUSE AND SPIRAX SARCO SITE

A COMMEMORATIVE PLAQUE to Dr Edward Jenner – unveiled at Alpha House, St George's
Road, in 1949 – incorrectly recorded that Jenner, 'discoverer of vaccination', lived there.
However, Jenner lived in St George's Place whenever he was in Cheltenham, and Alpha House
was actually owned by surgeon Thomas Cother during that time. In 1809 Jenner claimed
that he had successfully vaccinated between 3,000 and 4,000 people against smallpox in the
Cheltenham area during one epidemic and Alpha House, an old farmhouse known locally as the
'pest house', was certainly significant as the base for Jenner's ground-breaking work that year.

Alpha House had a more legitimate claim to fame, which has never been adequately
celebrated. Samuel Wilderspin, an untrained teacher from London, published *On the Importance
of Educating the Infant Poor* (1823), advocating that a teacher must become child-like himself in
order to be successful. The Revd Francis Close invited Wilderspin to Cheltenham to help set up an
infant school in Alstone. The school was a great success, but the men argued vehemently over
a second infant school in St James' in 1830, because Close insisted on a curriculum based on
scripture and rote-learning. Wilderspin defiantly set up an Infant School depot at Alpha House,
where he lived, lecturing on infant education across Britain, and supplying his newly founded
schools with books and equipment from the house until he moved to Dublin in 1839.

IN THE 1930s ALPHA HOUSE was neighbour to the Dingly Dell Candy factory, and later become part of Spirax Sarco Engineering, a company specialising in high quality products for the control of steam and other industrial fluids, which had moved its headquarters to Cheltenham in about 1945. In 2010 the company sold its site on St George's Road and, despite its unique history, Alpha House was demolished in 2011 to make way for a large McCarthy & Stone retirement development, expected to be completed in 2013.

CALCUTTA INN AND ST GEORGE'S GATE

DATING FROM THE 1830s, the Calcutta Inn stood at the corner of Gloucester Road and St George's Road, its architecture typical of many nineteenth-century corner public houses. Originally the lower half of the building had exposed locally-made brickwork in a chequered pattern of red and cream bricks, still to be seen in Calcutta Terrace (163–9 St George's Road) behind the site. The inn gave its name to the area around the road junction and 'Calcutta' appeared on bus timetables until very recently. The name is a reflection of Cheltenham's connections with India. From the late eighteenth century, military officers and civilian officials of the East India Company retired to Cheltenham as its sheltered location was said to provide a climate that was much like Simla, a hill station in north-eastern India that served as the summer capital for the British. Also the mild saline waters were particularly recommended as a palliative for tropical disease, liver conditions and digestive disorders.

THE CENTRAL PART OF THE BUILDING was always a public house, but small businesses occupied the outer sections. The St George's Road door led into the Gloucester Road post office from 1888 until 1915. In the 1920s and '30s Miss Prew kept a small sweet shop here; the post office had been moved around the corner to 116 Gloucester Road briefly, and then to the front room of 110 Gloucester Road where Sidney Spence was the sub-postmaster. The public house closed in the early 2000s, one of many that are disappearing from the town due to the economic downturn and changes in people's social life. The Calcutta Inn was demolished in 2003 and replaced in 2005 by the St George's Gate flats. Oddly the three-storey inn (the fourth storey was a sham with nothing behind the parapet) has been replaced with a five-storey block that bears no relation in scale or appearance to its neighbours.

LADIES'
COLLEGE BATHS

SWIMMING WAS POPULAR with Cheltenham Ladies'
College girls from as early as the 1880s, and they were
taken to the Montpellier Baths on 'clean-water' days. In
1911 their own large swimming pool was built in Malvern
Road near the school's sports field.

The pool could be boarded over in winter and used as a
gymnasium, and features included a visitors' gallery,
66 poolside changing cubicles, spray baths and a basement
laundry that kept swimmers supplied with warm, if
slightly board-like, towels. Wet bathing costumes were
posted down the laundry chute and returned to owners'
pigeonholes fully rinsed and dried. In the early days the
uniform bathing dress was black alpaca with a blue linen
yoke and monogram. A white cross was stitched on the
back when the girls were able to swim a length.

DURING THE SECOND WORLD WAR most Ladies' College buildings, including boarding houses, were commandeered, but the headmistress Miss Popham had the foresight to fill the pool with water, hoping the authorities would be unaware that the floor could be covered. She succeeded in saving the swimming pool for wartime college use and it became a hall housing four classes. Cubicles were used for private study, books and stationery were stored in the basement, the secretaries worked in the entrance hall and Miss Popham herself used the towel cupboard as a small office. Outside on the playing fields, sixteen army huts were erected, each providing two classrooms.

The Edwardian entrance hall was retained when the original swimming bath was replaced in 1994 by a modern 25m pool as part of the new Cheltenham Ladies' College Sports Centre, opened in 1995 by Olympic gold medallist Adrian Moorhouse. Facilities at the new sports centre include a weights theatre and two air-conditioned fitness suites, a sprung-floor sports hall for a variety of ball games, four squash courts and twenty-three all-weather tennis courts.

GWR ENGINE SHED
AND TRAVIS PERKINS

THE ALSTONE BRICK AND TILE WORKS on Gloucester Road, which made bricks from local clay for the booming nineteenth-century building trade, included a large dome-topped pottery kiln and three large drying sheds. John Williams and Co. bought the site in 1855 and modernised the brickmaking process by installing a steam pug mill for mixing the clay. The site proved a fatal attraction for John Young, a pupil at the nearby Christ Church Boys' School, who drowned while swimming with friends in the treacherous water-filled clay pits in 1864.

MALVERN ROAD STATION was opened on the same site by the Great Western Railway in 1908, allowing trains on the Stratford-upon-Avon line, which terminated at Cheltenham's St James' station, to turn around rather than doing their return journey in reverse. Malvern Road station closed in 1966, but the Cheltenham to Honeybourne stretch of line remained open for occasional freight traffic until 25 August 1976 when the derailment of a coal train at Winchcombe caused damage which was considered uneconomic to repair. A variety of buildings have been erected on the station site since the closure of the line. The southern area was developed by Cheltenham-based builders' merchants Sharpe & Fisher and taken over by Travis Perkins in 1999. Reminders of the site's railway past still exist at Travis Perkins; the large brick-built engine shed, shown in the earlier photograph, has been converted into a wood store, and the initials GWR can be seen on the original iron entrance gates. The remainder of the site has included a garage and petrol station, car showrooms (now a heating company) and most recently luxury flats.

The long roadway from Malvern Road, which provided the main public access to the station, today gives access to the Honeybourne Line Cycle Path, a popular route for walkers and cyclists between Cheltenham Spa station and Pittville Park along the route of the old track.

GLOUCESTER ROAD

GLOUCESTER ROAD is one of Cheltenham's busiest roads, as the earlier scene shows with the trams passing each other near the junction with Queens Road. The scene has outwardly changed very little today, although the traffic is modern and the buildings have undergone a change of use. The chapel in the centre was opened on 14 May 1891 as the first St Mark's Wesleyan Chapel. Prior to this, mission workers from Bethesda Methodist Church had held open-air services on Lansdown railway bridge from 1881. On 15 November 1911 the present St Mark's Methodist Church was officially opened on the opposite side of Gloucester Road. On 1 November 1981 the church held a commemorative service at the lamp at the road junction to celebrate a century of Methodism in the St Mark's district. The earlier chapel was used as a Methodist Sunday school for most of the last century, but has been converted for a number of commercial uses in recent years. It is currently a women's fitness centre, opened by TV handyman Tommy Walsh.

THE CORNER SHOP on the right of the picture was a bakery run by the Smith family for most of the twentieth century. There was a time when almost every street corner in Cheltenham housed a provisions store of some kind, but the days of the corner shop are in decline since development of edge-of-town supermarkets has changed our shopping habits forever. There is still one thriving corner shop remaining in Gloucester Road – Andrew's the newsagents at the Alstone Lane junction, but in order to survive it only closes on one day each year – Christmas Day. Over the last few decades the corner property at the Queens Road junction has been home to the Mini-Roundabout Chinese and Cantonese Takeaway, catering for the immediate neighbourhood, as well as travellers arriving at Cheltenham Spa station opposite.

TRAMS AND BUSES

PUBLIC TRANSPORT WITHIN CHELTENHAM was limited to two sedan chairs in 1781, available for hire at 6*d* per trip. Gradually wheelchairs and flys were introduced, then a larger fleet of hackney carriages. In June 1890 the first horse-drawn omnibus ran between Lansdown station (now Cheltenham Spa) and Pittville Gates for one penny. This short-lived venture was soon replaced by electric trams. The American tramway pioneer Thomas Nevins founded the Cheltenham & District Light Railway in 1898, and the initials CDLR can still be seen over a doorway at the present bus depot at Lansdown.

IT TOOK 120 MEN nearly four months to lay the 3ft 6ins gauge track, and the tramlines were set in wooden paving blocks supplied by the Acme Flooring & Paving Co. Occasionally, after heavy rain, blocks would swell and pop up out of the road, causing considerable consternation to road users. The first public tram ran from Lansdown to the top of Cleeve Hill on 22 August 1901 and the system was extended to Leckhampton and Charlton Kings in 1905. The trams were very popular, despite those ascending Cleeve Hill frequently towing trailers of horse manure from the town centre to be spread on the land.

Motor buses were introduced in 1912, finally replacing the electric trams in 1930–1. Most of the trams were scrapped, although a few were recycled in the local area. Fittingly one was converted to a bus shelter on the top of Cleeve Hill, while the No. 21 tram was used by a market gardener in Swindon Village as a store for 30 years. It was recovered in 1962, restored and sent to the National Tramway Museum in Crich, Derbyshire. It was returned to the town in 1992 and is being stored by Cheltenham Borough Council in the hope that it will one day be back on public display.

BLACK & WHITE
COACH STATION

IN JULY 1926 motor engineer George Readings set up a coach company offering tours of the
Cheltenham area. By 1928 Readings had twenty-one vehicles providing travel to London and other
destinations beyond Gloucestershire. Within two years the company, Black & White Motorways
Ltd, was the largest of its kind in Britain, with a fleet of forty coaches travelling to all parts of the
country. In 1930 Readings sold his successful business to the Bristol Tramways Co. and Midland
Red, although the name Black & White was retained.

THE EARLY COACHES were carpeted and curtained, with individual reading lamps and even vases on the window pillars. A steward catered for travellers' needs and dispensed drinks during the journey, to be safely enjoyed in the knowledge that there was even an onboard loo. Readings introduced black and white as the corporate livery, extending the theme throughout the business, including stationery and uniforms. However Black & White tactfully issued light grey uniforms to drivers running a new service to Paris in 1976, as the French authorities felt black and white uniforms would remind people of the SS and the Nazi Occupation.

By 1931 the Black & White Company had outgrown its original site, the former Diamond Laundry premises in Charlton Kings, and moved to St Margaret's in St Margaret's Road. The grand house was used as a ticket office until destroyed by a bomb in 1940. As part of the larger Associated Motorways, Cheltenham coach station became the hub of the nation's long-distance coach travel network. Every day at 2.00 p.m. there would be a mass exodus from the Black & White Coach Station and traffic would become grid-locked. Business gradually declined after the opening of the nearby M5 in 1970 and the coach station finally closed in 1986. The site has been used as a car park since then, awaiting development.

NORTH PLACE

NORTH PLACE ALE & PORTER STORES opened in 1852 on the corner of North Place and Northfield Passage, with William Halford as its first proprietor. After a series of owners, the Gay family took on the business in 1895. Harry Gay became landlord in 1931, the premises being known as Harry Gay's until closure in 1962. The 1960s photograph shows a Flowers Ales advertisement attached to the roof. On the right can be seen the bow front of Formosa House, formerly Grenville Cottage, which fills the angle between Northfield Terrace and Northfield Passage. This house now overlooks the Portland Street car park that has long been awaiting development. In 1815 this car park site was home to the Hunt Kennels serving the Cotswold Hunt, established in Cheltenham by Col. William Fitzhardinge Berkeley in 1809. Within a few years the kennels moved out to Whaddon Road.

THE AREA AROUND THE NORTH PLACE ALE & PORTER STORES was not without controversy; in April 1884 George Jew of Vine Cottage, Northfield Passage, was summonsed for keeping a disorderly house. The Revd J. Flory of Northfield Terrace, Minister of Bethel Chapel, gave evidence saying that for years past he had observed immoral conduct at Vine Cottage. In the previous month he had seen almost nude girls in a front room. There was laughter in court when the magistrate commented that Flory must have especially looked in through the window to witness this behaviour.

The terrace across the road from Harry Gay's was begun as early as 1819. It remained until about 1970 when all but one house were demolished; strangely No. 14 North Place was excluded from the compulsory purchase order placed on the rest of the terrace. No. 14 was finally removed in about 1980. There is currently (2012) a proposal to build apartments on the car park with a public open space in the middle.

VIEW FROM PITTVILLE PUMP ROOM

THE ENGRAVING (published by Johnson in 1846) purports to show the view across Cheltenham from the roof of Pittville Pump Room, but uses considerable artistic licence – the Pump Room dome is far too small to allow such a walkway around it. Holy Trinity Church can be seen in the centre of the engraving, the first Anglican building to supplement the parish church, designed by G.A. Underwood and opened in 1823. Over to the right is the spire of the parish church and on the far right is the tower of St Paul's Church, designed by the architect of Pittville Pump Room, John Forbes, in 1827. St Paul's was built in one of the poorer areas of town and provided free sittings for the congregation. In the distance, just to the right of Holy Trinity, is the chimney of the Montpellier Baths and Salts Manufactory, now the Playhouse. In the distance on the left is the spire of St Peter's Church, Leckhampton, and beyond that a mountainous cliff that is Johnson's representation of Leckhampton Hill. At that time the hill was still being actively quarried and so a considerable amount of bare rock could be clearly seen.

THE MODERN VIEW shows Pittville Park as it sweeps down to the ornamental lake, but Cheltenham is largely obscured by trees. The spire of St Mary's parish church can barely be seen on the far right, and Leckhampton Hill is straight ahead. Sadly its scree slopes and exposed rock faces, with much of the specific flora and fauna that it supported, have long gone, replaced by trees and scrub following the decline in quarrying. Now it looks quite featureless when viewed across the town from Pittville. The modern photograph does show Cheltenham's location in the shelter of the Cotswold scarp, providing the microclimate that attracted ex-colonials to retire here during the nineteenth century.

PITTVILLE PARK

PITTVILLE PARK – Cheltenham's largest ornamental park – was opened in 1825 as part of the 100-acre development by Joseph Pitt between 1825 and 1830 to the north of the town. Pitt's vision was for an estate of 500 to 600 houses accommodating wealthy residents whom he hoped would settle in the 'new town' of Pittville. Visitors to Cheltenham were encouraged to visit Pittville Pump Room, which opened in 1830, to take the waters.

IT IS OFTEN THOUGHT that Pittville, and other parks, such as Montpellier, were only used by residents and visitors who could afford the subscriptions, for rides, promenades and other genteel pastimes. However, these areas were popular venues for many larger events in the town, which members of the wider public were able to attend. The engraving, published by the *Illustrated London News*, is of the twelfth annual exhibition of the County of Gloucester Agricultural Society, held in Pittville Park in September 1867. Reported nationally, it appears to have been a lively and very noisy event; horses and sheep were displayed, cheeses and vegetable produce were shown, and agricultural implements – including steam-driven machinery – were demonstrated. Another more unusual entertainment was the Aquatic Carnival held in Pittville Lake by Cheltenham Swimming and Water Polo Club in June 1911. Cheltenham played water polo against Stroud and Gloucester, winning both games 2–0, and the event also included swimming and diving competitions, a lifesaving demonstration, and a 'comic sketch'.

In 1900 residents complained of the noise made by Pittville's free-roaming peacocks, and some even requested they be shot. Aviaries were first erected here in about 1936 as part of a move to attract visitors to Pittville Park, considered by many to be too far out of town. By 1941 the collection included a pair of ravens, and the feeding of the Pittville Park birds, rabbits and other animals is a fond childhood memory for many who have grown up in Cheltenham.

LIFEBOATS ON PITTVILLE LAKE

A LIFEBOAT WAS AT THE CENTRE of one of the most spectacular public events to take place in the town during the nineteenth century. Funded by the people of Cheltenham and surrounding area for the Royal National Lifeboat Institution (RNLI), the lifeboat was brought from London to Cheltenham by train on 10 October 1866 and paraded triumphantly through the streets of the town. The *Illustrated London News* reported that 'Dense crowds of people filled the streets and occupied every doorstep and position whence a good view could be commanded. The procession must have been over half a mile in length.' Lady Charlotte Schreiber, wife of the town's MP, named the vessel *The Cheltenham Lifeboat*. The 32ft vessel with ten oars was then launched onto Pittville Lake, manned by a crew of sailors in the latest cork life jackets, who rowed several times around the lake to the tune of 'Rule Britannia'. The lifeboat was then deliberately capsized, but quickly righted herself to the 'vociferous cheers of thousands'. There was another hearty reception when the lifeboat arrived at Burnham-on-Sea, and a Cheltenham deputation participated in her launch there. She became the first lifeboat to serve the busy Bristol Channel shipping trade, and remained at Burnham until 1887, saving thirty-six lives.

HISTORY REPEATED ITSELF when a modern inflatable inshore lifeboat, manned by four members of the present Burnham-on-Sea crew, was launched in front of Pittville Pump Room on 4 March 2012. The launch was to publicise a new play performed later that month at the award-winning Parabola Arts Centre, Cheltenham Ladies' College, to raise funds for the RNLI. *Out of the Mist*, written by Gloucestershire-based playwright Alan Tyson, explores 'the humour, sadness, triumph and disaster that RNLI volunteers have experienced' since the organisation was first formed in 1824. The successful two-day run was directed by Jenny Wicks of Cheltenham's Everyman Theatre.

BRIDGE AT PITTVILLE PARK

IN ABOUT 1810 the old mill and millpond, which once stood at the western end of what is now Pittville Park, became part of the estate belonging to Marle Hill House, built for Robert Capper, a wealthy local lawyer, magistrate and JP. In 1892 the Cheltenham Corporation purchased much of the estate and neighbouring land, allowing them to extend Capper's Pond. The corporation also purchased Pittville Pump Room and Gardens, east of the Evesham Road, and several other pieces of land from the bankrupt Pittville Estate. In 1894 the entire area on both sides of the Evesham Road became Pittville Park.

In 1893 a rustic bamboo bridge was built approximately where a bridge across Wyman's Brook, at the eastern end of Capper's Pond, had formed part of the footpath between Marle Hill House and Cheltenham. Since that time there have been a number of wooden bridges on this site, the last of which was constructed by the Royal Engineers, but was sadly destroyed by vandals in 2004.

REINSTATING THE BRIDGE was the most popular proposal when Cheltenham residents were asked for their views on projects to regenerate Pittville Park in 2009. Cheltenham artist and blacksmith Christopher Lisney, who crafts garden sculpture in steel for exhibition and sale both in the UK and abroad, and shows at the Chelsea Flower Show annually, was commissioned to produce a new design. The galvanised metal bridge has provoked considerable debate. Over sixty people witnessed the opening of the Pittville Community Bridge on 9 February 2012. The bridge, which incorporates ideas by pupils from nearby Dunalley Primary School, cost £145,000 and was co-funded by Cheltenham Borough Council and the Severn Trent Flood Relief Fund. The fund was set up following the floods that devastated much of Gloucestershire, including Cheltenham and Pittville Park, in 2007.

PAGEANT AND DRAGON
BOATS AT PITTVILLE

PAGEANTS WERE POPULAR FORMS OF ENTERTAINMENT during the Edwardian period, with large casts enacting historical scenes with great patriotic fervour. Cheltenham was selected to host the Gloucestershire Historical Pageant in 1908 because of its 'admirable advantages for scenic effects, the accommodation it affords its visitors, and its excellent railway communication'.
The pageant was performed between 6 and 11 July 1908 in Pittville Park and on the boating lake in front of Marle Hill House with the aim of raising funds for Boer War veterans. The Baring Brothers, local entrepreneurs, were the event managers, and the script was written by actor, playwright and Pageant Master George P. Hawtrey. Many local county families and commercial firms gave their patronage and support.

The Cheltenham pageant was 'a brilliant spectacle', with 3,000 players and 300 horses performing eight 'historical episodes', beginning with 'The Capture of Caractacus' and ending with King George III's visit to Cheltenham in 1788. The chorus, who principally represented the rivers Thames, Severn (Sabrina), Avon (Avona) and Chelt, rowed in boats on the lake, singing and explaining the action. The event was deemed a great success and in 1909 the Baring Brothers were appointed Managers of the Bath Pageant. Hawtrey went on to become Master of the Welsh Pageant in Cardiff in 1909, and the Chester Pageant in 1910.

DRAGON BOAT RACING was held on Pittville boating lake in 2003 to mark the fiftieth anniversary of the Samaritans charity and the fortieth anniversary of the Cheltenham branch. The event, entitled 'Dragons on the Lake', was organised by Cheltenham Friends of the Samaritans, and sponsored by the Summerfield Trust and many others, raising over £11,000. The Friends of the Samaritans celebrated their own twenty-fifth anniversary with a second dragon boat race in 2004, and held the event a third time in 2005. In total 'Dragons' raised over £25,000 for the Cheltenham Samaritans.

THE RACECOURSE
AND THE CENTAUR

THE FIRST ORGANISED Cheltenham horse race took place on Nottingham Hill in 1815, but it was not until August 1818 that a more formal meet took place. In 1819 a 3-mile course was opened on Cleeve Hill, with an impressive grandstand visible from the Promenade. The first Gold Cup race took place that year with a substantial prize of 100 guineas. The races became an annual event, to the horror of the Revd Francis Close who railed against its evils. In 1830 the grandstand mysteriously burned down, and the event moved to Prestbury Park, where the first steeplechase took place in 1834. From 1853 to 1898 the event occupied various temporary sites, including the old Gloucester Road near Fiddler's Green, before returning to Prestbury Park where a permanent course was first laid out in 1902.

During the First World War a VAD (Voluntary Aid Detachment) hospital was set up at the racecourse, receiving wounded Belgian soldiers on 28 October 1914, followed by British, Canadian and then French casualties from the trenches. At the beginning of the Second World War the Royal Gloucestershire Hussars were stationed at the racecourse, where there was plenty of room for them to practise manoeuvring tanks, but very limited accommodation. The soldiers had to sleep in the stables, moving out during the races that continued throughout the war.

THE CENTAUR OPENED at Prestbury Park in 2004, one of the largest auditoria in the South West. It is a multi-purpose facility with a seating capacity for 2,000, and a standing capacity of 4,000. The Centaur can host conferences, concerts, dinners, exhibitions, shows and large private parties, and in 2007 it brought the West End musical *Cats* to the town. Stars who have performed at the venue include Jools Holland, Elaine Paige and Russell Watson. The Centaur also hosts the annual Greenbelt festival, the largest Christian arts and music festival in the world.

GCHQ AT OAKLEY

OAKLEY FARM WAS FAMED in Cheltenham as early as 1903, when Colonel W.F. Cody, otherwise known as Buffalo Bill, put on his spectacular show there. Four trains hauling sixty carriages brought his 500 showmen to the town, and nearly 20,000 people attended the performances at Oakley.

In 1939 the War Office built distinctive single-storey blocks at Oakley Farm, east of Cheltenham, and Benhall Farm, west of the town, to accommodate staff evacuated from London and south-east England. Soon afterwards, the US Army's Services of Supply occupied the sites as their headquarters before moving to France in 1944, to be replaced by the UK Ministry of Pensions. The Government Code and Cypher School, renamed Government Communications Headquarters (GCHQ) in 1946, moved from Eastcote, London, to Cheltenham in 1952. Known locally as the 'Foreign Office', GCHQ was a mystery to most people in Cheltenham for years. However, in 1982 the trial of Geoffrey Prime, a GCHQ linguist and Russian spy, raised public awareness, and in 1983 the department's role was acknowledged for the first time. The Trade Unions ban at GCHQ from 1984 to 1997 aroused considerable debate.

TODAY GCHQ'S SIGNALS INTELLIGENCE WORK provides information to support government decision-making on international issues, such as the Gulf War. Increasingly intelligence is also used to combat terrorism, and to detect and prevent serious crime. CESG, the Information Assurance arm of GCHQ, also protects the UK's vital interests by providing policy and assistance on the security of online communications and electronic data across government, the health service and other essential services. In the early twenty-first century a radical, circular building was constructed at Benhall to house the workforce more effectively and economically. The 'Doughnut' was fully occupied by 2004, and the Oakley site finally closed in December 2011, sixty years after GCHQ first moved to Cheltenham. The lower part of the site has been redeveloped as housing and a supermarket, shown here in 2011.

INDEX